Module 7: Referencing & Avoiding Plagiarism

Introduction

This module has been written to both raise your awareness of, and instruct you in, the conventions of citing in academic writing, the mechanics of creating bibliographies and issues surrounding plagiarism. The tasks in each unit are designed in such a way that you move from micro-tasks to more holistic activities, bringing together all that has been covered in the unit. By the end of this module, you should feel more confident about the difficult and thorny academic task of incorporating researched material into your own writing, with your own voice.

Contents

Defining plagiarism

At the end of this unit, you will be able to:

- understand key terminology
- understand what constitutes plagiarism
- discuss why students might plagiarise
- understand what constitutes common knowledge

According to Carroll (2002) 'plagiarism is passing off someone's work, whether intentionally or unintentionally, as your own, for your own benefit' (p. 9).

Task 1 Defining key terminology

1.1 There is some important terminology that you need to understand as it will be used throughout this module. Match the words (a–i) with the appropriate definition (1–9).

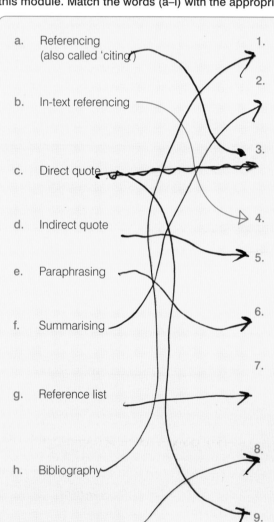

a. Referencing (also called 'citing')

b. In-text referencing

c. Direct quote

d. Indirect quote

e. Paraphrasing

f. Summarising

g. Reference list

h. Bibliography

i. Plagiarism

1. A list placed at the end of your work of all the resources cited in your work.

2. Paraphrasing or summarising the work of an author and placing it in your academic work without quotation marks, but with an acknowledgement.

3. Acknowledging someone else's ideas, words or work through both in-text referencing and a reference list or bibliography (end-text).

4. The use of direct and indirect quotes within the text of your document.

5. A brief account of someone else's ideas or words, highlighting the main points and leaving out the details.

6. Converting someone else's ideas or words into your own words through substitutions.

7. A complete list of all the resources you have referred to in your work as well as resources you may have used to help develop your thoughts, but which you have not cited in your work.

8. The use of the published or unpublished work of another person without full acknowledgement both in-text and end-of-text.

9. Placing someone else's words in your academic writing within quotation marks and acknowledging the author.

Task 2 Defining plagiarism

2.1 **Read the extended definition of *plagiarism*. Complete the sentences using the words in the box.**

reproducing	Sciences	person's	modifications	origins
communication	expressed	pretence	acknowledge	

The word 'plagiarism' has its ᵃ_____ in the Latin language where it meant 'thief'.

Plagiarism covers a wide range of situations from failing to ᵇ_____ adequately the sources you have used, to whole-scale copying.

These sources may include published work, websites or verbal ᶜ_____.

Some students produce a 'patchwork' effect in their academic writing by ᵈ_____ shorter lines or phrases perhaps with minor ᵉ_____ and linking them together in the ᶠ_____ that these are their own ideas ᵍ_____ in their own words.

In the ʰ_____, plagiarism may take the form of copying another ⁱ_____ results, calculations or programme codes, perhaps with minor changes in accuracy, explanation, layout or identifiers.

2.2 **Study the eight examples. Do they amount to plagiarism? Discuss with a partner which you think is the most serious form of plagiarism and why.**

a. Sarah paid £100 for an essay over the internet, complete with in-text references and a bibliography, and handed it in as her own work.

b. John used ideas and words from external sources as part of his essay, but did not acknowledge the authors either in-text or in the bibliography.

c. Mohammed used ideas and words from external sources as part of his essay, but only acknowledged the authors in the bibliography.

d. Mei Mei found some useful information on an anonymous website so reproduced it verbatim in her essay and passed it off as her own idea.

e. Teddy used data collected by another student through laboratory experiments and used the results to write his own laboratory report.

f. Professor Smith used data collected by a research student in a journal article he was writing, but he did not acknowledge the student.

g. Professor Bartholomew used some ideas which emerged from a discussion with a colleague in the lecture she gave to her undergraduate students, but did not mention that they were her colleague's ideas.

h. Johannes copied a design from a magazine and used it as part of a painting he was doing for his degree show.

Task 3 Why do students plagiarise?

3.1 There are many reasons why a student might plagiarise. Discuss which of the reasons given below is the most likely in your opinion. Can you think of any other explanations?

    a.   Not having enough time to construct a proper piece of academic writing because of several deadlines falling at the same time, so putting together a patchwork essay, using one's own and others' ideas, but not acknowledging the writers.

    b.   Not caring about constructing a proper piece of academic writing, so copying large sections from various books without acknowledgement and changing a few words here and there.

    c.   Not understanding the conventions for citing others' work within a piece of academic writing.

    d.   Being afraid of criticism for having too many direct quotations, so leaving out some of the quotation marks in the hope that it can be passed off as one's own work.

-     _____

-     _____

3.2 There are many reasons why a student should not plagiarise. Discuss with a partner the most compelling argument against plagiarising. Can you think of any other reasons?

    a.   It is against the university/college rules and regulations and could result in a loss of marks or even – at worst – expulsion from the university.

    b.   It is against the law. In the 18th century, laws were introduced in Britain to protect 'intellectual property' in addition to 'physical property'. 'Intellectual property' is defined by *Webster's Dictionary* as: 'Property that derives from the work of the mind or intellect; an idea, invention, trade secret, process, data, formula, patent, copyright or trademark.'

    c.   It is not nice to deceive your teachers and fellow students by passing off someone else's work as your own.

    d.   It is more satisfactory and a better learning experience to develop one's own ideas, supported by the work of authorities in the field. Citing others' work within your own writing is accepted academic practice and shows that you are a member of the academic community.

    e.   By citing sources properly you can be helpful to other academics. By citing a particular author in your work, you may be enhancing that individual's position within the academic world. Many academics measure their success in terms of how many times their work is cited in other people's work (list of citations).

-     _____

-     _____

Task 4 Identifying common knowledge

A reasonably educated person will know that 'the UN' stands for 'the United Nations', that Mars is covered in red deserts and that Christopher Columbus discovered America (to the West) in 1492. These facts are what is known as 'common knowledge', and would not normally need to be cited in your work.

However, people might not know such facts as the percentage of women under 21 years of age who voted in the last general election in the UK or the number of whales beached in Australia in 2013. Such facts are more obscure and will have come from others' research; the authors of these works will need to be given credit and cited in your own work.

What is and is not 'common knowledge' may also differ from subject to subject. That the chemical which makes plants green is chlorophyll is common knowledge to biologists, but may not be so to people who have studied other subjects. Such issues will influence your decision as to whether or not a citation is necessary.

4.1 **Mark the statements common knowledge (C), needs to be cited (N) or citation depends on the discipline (D).**

a. The novel *Animal Farm* was written by George Orwell. ☐

b. George Orwell's real name was in fact Eric Blair. ☐

c. Rivers grow larger as they make their way to the sea. ☐

d. Desertification is the extension of desert conditions into areas where deserts did not previously exist. ☐

e. In 2012, the USA had by far the highest number of road fatalities of any country, at 41,967. ☐

f. The peanut is not actually a nut, but belongs to the bean family. ☐

g. There is a correlation between supply and demand for any commodity. ☐

h. The ozone layer is being destroyed by pollution. ☐

i. The ozone is most concentrated 20–30 km above the Earth, in the upper atmosphere, and it filters ultraviolet light. ☐

j. The family is not a voluntary unit based on love and choice, but an economic unit which creates and maintains female dependence. ☐

1

4.2 List three things which you think are common knowledge in your subject area and show them to a student from another subject area to see if he/she is familiar with the ideas.

a. _____

b. _____

c. _____

Reflect

Write about the implications of one of the cases below.

a. A writer submitted an idea for a book to a publishing company, which turned the idea down. A few months later, a book came out which followed the writer's storyline almost exactly.

b. A scientist presented a treatment for diabetes at an international conference based on data that he had copied from someone else in his laboratory.

c. Students at a particular university had been buying essays over the internet and getting away with it until a journalist found out and wrote about it in a national newspaper.

At the end of this unit, you will:

- understand the purpose of a reference list and bibliography
- be able to produce a reference list and bibliography using the APA system

Task 1 Reference list or bibliography?

Referencing is the way writers state which sources they have used in a piece of work. Details of these sources are often found at the end of the piece of work in a reference list or bibliography. The entries are listed in alphabetical order.

1.1 **Work with a partner to discuss the questions. Share your answers with the class.**

a. What is the purpose of a reference list?

b. What is the difference between a *reference list* and a *bibliography*?

c. What type of publications often use reference lists and which tend to use bibliographies?

d. Why may an author choose to include a bibliography instead of a reference list?

e. Are you more likely to use a reference list or a bibliography in a presentation?

References

Bain, K. (2005). *Critical Thinking and Technology.* Retrieved from http://www. bestteachersinstitute.org/id98.html

Clemmons, R. (2013). Technology, Instruction and the 21st Century Classroom. *EdTech Magazine.* Retrieved from http://www.edtechmagazine.com/higher/article/2013/05/ technology-instruction-and-21st-century-classroom

Crawford, E. and Kirby, M. (2008). Fostering Students' Global Awareness: Technology applications in social studies teaching and learning. *Journal of Curriculum and Instruction, 2*(1), 56–73.

Dörnyei, Z. (2001). *Teaching and Researching Motivation.* England: Pearson Education Limited.

Friedman, T. L. (2005). *The world is flat: A brief history of the twenty-first century.* New York: Farrar, Straus and Giroux.

Guilloteaux, J. and Dörnyei, Z. (2008). Motivating Language Learners: A Classroom-Oriented Investigation of the Effects of Motivational Strategies on Student Motivation. *TESOL Quarterly, 42*(1), 55–77.

Hutchinson, T. and Waters, A. (1987). *English for Specific Purposes, a Learning-Centered Approach.* Cambridge: Cambridge University Press.

Infographic. (n.d.). *Components of the 21st Century Classroom.* Retrieved from http://www. opencolleges.edu.au/infographic/21st_century_classroom.html

Jordan, R. R. (2012). *English for academic purposes: A guide and resource book for teachers.* Cambridge, UK: Cambridge University Press.

Task 2 The APA style for referencing

The format used in referencing follows strict guidelines, which vary according to the system used. The system used here is one developed by the American Psychological Association, known as the APA System.

Referencing a book

The general APA referencing format is:

Author, A. A. (year). *Title of book* (XX ed., Vol XX). Location: Publisher.

> Example
> Sadava, D. E., Hillis, D. M., Heller, H. C., & Berenbaum, M. R. (2011). *Life: The Science of Biology* (9th ed., Vol. 1). Sunderland, MA: W. H. Freeman & Co.

2.1 Arrange the components of a book reference in the correct order.

International Political Economy	T. H.	(2012).	(5th ed.).
London,	Oatley,	England:	Longman.

Referencing a chapter in a book

The general APA referencing format is:

Author, A. A., & Author, B. B. (year). Title of chapter. In A. A. Editor, B. B. Editor, & C. C. Editor (Eds.), *Title of book* (pp. XXX–XXX). Location: Publisher.

> Example
> Smith, R. F., Gray, S. D., & Dale, W. S. (2004). Delay damages. In R. R. Cushman (Ed.), *Construction Business Handbook* (pp. 417–467). New York, NY: Aspen Publishers.

2.2 Study the example above and answer the questions.

a. How does the format for referencing a chapter differ to referencing a whole book?

Title of chapter

b. What does the *Ed.* stand for?

Editor

Journals are an excellent source of articles on current research and reviews of a subject. They are increasingly accessed online, but libraries still keep large stocks of printed journals, many of which cannot be accessed online. It is important therefore to know how to reference printed journal articles.

Referencing a journal article

The general APA referencing format is:
Author, A. A., & Author, B. B. (year). Title of article. *Title of journal, volume number*(issue number), XXX–XXX.

Example
Leadbeater, C., McIver, L., Campopiano, C. J., Webster, S. P., Baxter, R. L., Kelly S. M., & Wunro, A. W. (2000). Probing the NASPH-binding site of *Escherichia coli* flavodoxin oxidoreductase. *Biochemical Journal, 352*, 257–266.

2.3 **Study the example above and answer the questions.**

a. What is the title of the article?

Probing the NASPH-binding site of Escherichia coli Flavodoxin ....

b. How many authors does this article have?

7 (listed)

c. What is the name of the journal?

~~Escherichia coli flavodoxin oxidoreductase~~ Biochemical Journal

d. What does the *352* stand for?

volume number

e. What does *257–266* mean?

page / issue number

2.4 Many journals also use issue numbers and these should be included in the reference if the page numbering for each issue begins at 1.

Give the general format for a hard copy of a periodical, which includes journals, magazines, newspapers and newsletters, for three authors.

a. _____

b. _____

c. _____

2.5 Write a reference for the article below.

World Development Vol. 66, pp. 707–718, 2015
0305-750X/Crown Copyright 2014 Published by Elsevier Ltd.

doi:10.1016/j.worlddev.2014.09.028

NGOs, States, and Donors Revisited: Still Too Close for Comfort?

NICOLA BANKS [a], DAVID HULME [a], MICHAEL EDWARDS [b]

[a] *The University of Manchester, UK*
[b] *Open Democracy and Demos, Swan Lake, USA*

Summary – Serious questions remain about the ability of NGOs to meet long-term transformative goals in their work for development and social justice. We investigate how, given their weak roots in civil society and the rising tide of technocracy that has swept through the world of foreign aid, most NGOs remain poorly placed to influence the real drivers of social change. However we also argue that NGOs can take advantage of their traditional strengths to build bridges between grassroots organizations and local and national-level structures and processes, applying their knowledge of local contexts to strengthen their roles in empowerment and social transformation.

Key words: NGOs; civil society; poverty; development; foreign aid.

1. INTRODUCTION

In 1996 we wrote in World Development about our concerns regarding the impact of foreign aid on non-governmental organizations, arguing that despite donors investing heavily in development NGOs in order to strengthen good governance agendas and find an efficient channel for filling gaps in service delivery, these comparative advantages were based on ideological grounds rather than evidence. In fact, the increased dependence of NGOs on donor funding served to undermine the strengths that justified an increased role for NGOs in development (Hulme & Edwards, 1996). That these questions remain pertinent today was underlined when our recent working paper on the subject (see Banks & Hulme, 2012) was criticized by Duncan Green on his From Poverty to Power blog for being a 'generalized and ill-informed attack on NGOs'. The debate that followed, with contributions from academics, NGO practitioners and interested members of civil society, was picked up by an article on The Guardian's Global Development website,[1] which asked whether a fault-line was deepening between NGOs that are increasingly vocal about the problems they face and those who (at least publicly) remain passive or defensive.

Clearly we are at a point in the NGO debate at which serious questions are being raised about the ability of NGOs to meet their long-term goals of social justice and transformation at a time when the development sector is narrowly focused on short-term results and value for money. After two decades of research we are better-positioned to revisit these issues given the expanding depth and breadth of academic knowledge about NGOs, but we have yet to find a forum through which to bridge the gap that exists between NGOs and academics on this contentious subject: a space in which these issues can be discussed, debated, and deliberated through a process of collaboration and creative dialog, rather than through collision, avoidance, or mutual suspicion.

The NGO landscape has transformed dramatically in scale and profile since NGOs became prominent actors in development after the end of the Cold War. NGOs are bigger, more numerous and sophisticated, and receive a larger slice of foreign aid and other forms of development finance than ever before (AbouAssi, 2012, Africa, 2013, Brautigam and Segarra, 2007, Brown et al., 2007b, Clarke, 1998, Fisher, 1997 and Thomas, 2008). Other global transformations since the late 1990s have also influenced the capacities and strategies of NGOs. Rapid globalization and the spread of market liberalizing reforms across the Global South have led to the increasing influence of non-state actors on development policy and practice. We have also witnessed a staggering rise in inequality and the concentration of economic and political power in the hands of a small proportion of the world's richest countries and people (Houtzager, 2005). Alongside the rollback of welfare states we have seen the emergence of emerging powers (Brazil, India, and China), emerging middle powers (South Africa, Turkey, Indonesia, and others), large philanthrocapitalists and private donors (Herzer & Nunnenkamp, 2013) and new actors and alliances for development (Richey & Ponte, 2014).

Task 3 Referencing sources accessed online

Books and journals are increasingly accessed online, and university subscriptions to certain journals may allow you free access. When referencing online sources, it is important to include information that enables others to also access them online.

In recent years, journals have started including a digital object identifier (DOI) for their articles. Each DOI is a unique reference to the specific article and each DOI begins with '10' followed by a string of characters.

However, when including the DOI in a reference, the format to use is: http://dx.doi.org/10.xxx where xxx represents the rest of the DOI string.

Referencing a journal article online with DOI assigned

Author, A. A., & Author, B. B. (year). Title of article. *Title of Journal, volume number* (issue number) XXX–XXX. http://dx.doi.org/10.0000/0000 (or doi:0000000/000000000)

Example

Robinson, P. K., & Rainbird, H. (2013). International Supply Chains and the Labour Process. *Competition & Change, 17*(1), 91–107. http://dx.doi.org/10.1179/1024529412Z.00000000027

3.1 Write a reference for the online article below.

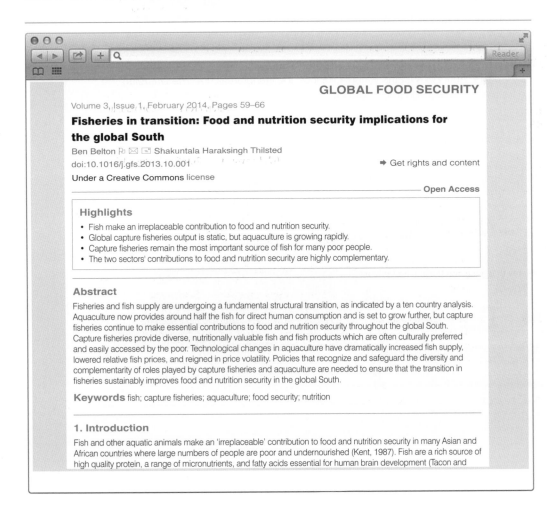

A uniform resource locator (URL) is the website address that can be copied from the browser window and pasted into the reference. When there is no DOI, state the URL of the website from which the source was retrieved. Use the URL of the journal homepage or, if retrieved elsewhere, give the URL of the article itself.

Examples

- Conversi, D. (2010). The Limits of Cultural Globalisation? *Journal of Critical Globalisation Studies, 3*, 36–59. Retrieved from http://www.criticalglobalisation.com/
- Copland, C. (2012). Show or tell? Video for living and learning. *Inform, 10*, 9–10. Retrieved from http://language-centre.sllf.qmul.ac.uk/sites/default/files/Inform-Issue-10.pdf

---

3.2 Study the examples above and then answer the questions.

a. Which of the two articles above was retrieved from the journal website and which from an alternative website?

_____

b. Why is it preferred to include the DOI in a reference when it exists, rather than the URL?

_____

c. Magazine articles are referenced in the same way as journals. Why?

_____

3.3 Most national newspapers have active websites which publish regular articles. These are referenced in a similar way to journals, but there are differences. Study the example below and discuss the similarities and differences of newspaper and journal references when accessed online.

Example

Ravilious, K. (2014, April 20). Weatherwatch: Like it or not, the future is hot. *The Guardian.* Retrieved from http://www.theguardian.com/uk

---

Task 4 Referencing articles on websites

Online sources, such as corporate websites, may publish articles which you choose to use in your work. You should, however, be cautious, ensuring the source is suitably reliable for your work.

The general referencing format for webpages is as follows:

Referencing a webpage
The general APA referencing format is: Author, A. A. (year). Title of document [Format]. Retrieved from http://xxxxx

Where the URL does not clearly state the name of the website, for example, where the name appears as an abbreviation, the website name (company, institute or organisation name), should be included in the retrieval statement. The article name is not put in italics unless it is a stand-alone report.

4.1 **Study the examples of references to articles on websites where the author is named and answer the questions.**

> Examples
> • Harrison, A. (2011). Vocational education not good enough, says Wolf report. Retrieved from British Broadcasting Corporation News website: http://www.bbc.co.uk/news/education-12622061
> • Smith, J. (2013). 10 ways to be more confident at work. Retrieved from http://www.forbes.com/sites/jacquelynsmith/2013/03/05/10-ways-to-be-more-confident-at-work/
> • Johnson, S. B. (2012). *APA President's Report August 2012 Council of Representatives*. Retrieved from American Psychological Association website: http://www.apa.org/about/governance/president/report-august-2012.pdf

a. In Harrison (2011), why is 'British Broadcasting Corporation News website' stated, whereas, in Smith (2013), the website name 'Forbes' is not given in the retrieval statement?

_____

_____

b. Why is the document title put in italics in Johnson (2012), but not for Smith (2013) or Harrison (2011)?

_____

_____

4.2 Now study the following reference examples where an article is published by an organisation or the article has no named authors and answer the questions.

> **Examples**
>
> • Creative Education. (2014, May 21). How To Make Team Teaching Work [Blog post]. Retrieved from http://www.creativeeducation.co.uk/blog/index.php/2014/05/make-team-teaching-work/
>
> • American Psychological Association. (2013). *Managing chronic pain: How psychologists can help with pain management.* Retrieved from http://www.apa.org/helpcenter/pain-management.aspx
>
> • US economy contracted in first quarter of 2014. (2014). Retrieved from British Broadcasting Corporation News website: http://www.bbc.co.uk/news/business-27616183

a. Why is the month and day given in Creative Education (2014)?

_____

b. The abbreviation 'apa' of the website name 'American Psychological Association' is given in the URL of American Psychological Association (2013). Why then is the organisation name not also given in the retrieval information as it was for Johnson, S. B. (2012) in Task 4.1?

_____

c. Why is the BBC not stated as a corporate author in 'US economy contracted in first quarter of 2014' (2014)?

_____

d. Describe the format of a reference for which no author is given.

_____

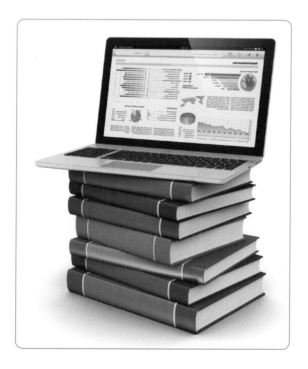

Task 5 Further resources

There are a great many different sources available online and within libraries, including television programmes, online videos, radio recordings, legal and government documents, and more. You can find out how to reference different types of sources using some of the sources presented in the bibliography for this unit (see below). Be careful to note that the rules for the APA format change with time and currently the most up-to-date rules are the APA 6th edition rules.

Bibliography

American Psychological Association. (2010). *Publication manual of the American Psychological Association* (6th ed.). Washington, DC: American Psychological Association.

American Psychological Association. (2012). *APA style guide to electronic references* [PDF version]. Retrieved from http://www.apastyle.org/products/4210512.aspx

Lee, C. (2010, November 18). How to cite something you found on a website in APA style [Blog post]. Retrieved from http://blog.apastyle.org/apastyle/2010/11/how-to-cite-something-you-found-on-a-website-in-apa-style.html

Stefanie. (2012, January 5). Got volume [Blog post]. Retrieved from http://blog.apastyle.org/apastyle/2012/01/got-volume.html

5.1 Discuss with the class any new formatting present in the bibliography and decide on the rules for this formatting.

Reflect

Think about the kind of sources you are likely to use in your work and how you will reference them.

Which examples in this unit will be most useful and where can you find examples of sources that are not shown here?

At what stage in your work is it most helpful to write a reference list or bibliography and why is it important for it to be complete?

3 The mechanics of citations

At the end of this unit, you will be able to:

- use direct and indirect quotations or citations in your writing
- understand the differences between paraphrasing and summarising

Task 1 When to use citations?

1.1 Which of the following would you need to reference and why?

a. words copied from a book or article

b. facts found in a book

c. your own idea

d. a diagram found on the internet

e. an idea from another book/article

f. common knowledge

g. word-of-mouth communication

Direct quotations involve the use of an author's exact words, which are placed inside quotation marks to indicate that they are someone else's words. In addition, it must be clear to the reader who the words belong to and in which source they appear. As a rule, direct quotations are used less often than citations.

1.2 Read the direct quotation example. Work with a partner to answer the questions.

> Bibliographical entry for the source:
> Szasz, T. S. (1974). *The Second Sin*. New York: Routledge & Kegan Paul.

While modern medicine has been able to find cures for many of the diseases which would in the past have killed or maimed many, it is still the case that medicine does not have all the answers. Nevertheless, people's faith in a doctor's ability to cure is strong and physicians are treated as gods or demi-gods by many. **Szasz (1974)** comments that, "Formerly, when religion was strong and science weak, men mistook magic for medicine; now, when science is strong and religion weak, men mistake medicine for magic" (p. 124).

a. Why did the essay writer decide to quote, rather than paraphrase, Szasz?

b. Which words are from Szasz's book? How do you know?

c. Is Szasz the author's first or last name?

d. Why doesn't the essay writer include Szasz's initials (T. S.)?

e. Which words are the essay writer's own words?

f. Why has the essay writer included *1974* in brackets?

g. What does *p. 124* mean and why has the essay writer included this information?

Task 2 Reasons for using direct quotations

2.1 Read the explanation about when to use direct quotations. Complete the sentences using the words in the box.

misrepresentation	vivid	easier	summarised

Direct quotations tend to be used when the author has used particularly
a_____ or well-phrased language which cannot be b_____
without losing some of the impact of the original words. They may also be used when there
is a wish to avoid any ambiguity or c_____ of the source material. Direct
quotes are not used because it is d_____ to copy an author's words than to
try expressing them in your own voice.

Task 3 Longer direct quotations: block style

3.1 Read the excerpt from an article about the challenges students face with regards to referencing, and answer the questions below.

> In adjusting to post-secondary education, written assignments present challenges for many students. As Laidley (2010) indicates:
>
> Students need to develop an understanding of the academic literacy requirements of their chosen field, including discourse organisation ... and the appropriate acknowledgement of references. Such expectations may not be obvious to many students unless explicitly pointed out to them. (p. 76)

a. How is the layout of a long quotation different from that of a short quotation?

_____

_____

b. Why has the essay writer used three dots?

_____

_____

c. What do you notice about the placement of the page number?

_____

_____

d. Is there any maximum length for a direct quotation? What might that be?

_____

_____

e. Why isn't it considered good style to have too many block quotations in an essay?

_____

_____

Task 4 Choosing what to quote directly

4.1 Which of the following would you keep as a direct quotation (DQ)? Why/Why not?

a. Albert Einstein talking about education: _____

'I never teach my pupils.
I only attempt to provide the
conditions in which they can learn.'

b. Edward Sapir talking about the relationship between culture and language: _____

'It is a well-known and undisputed fact that languages
differ in the number of basic colour terms they have,
some languages having a few as four terms.'

c. Confucius talking about history: _____

'Study the past if you would define the future.'

d. William Harvey talking about the human circulatory system: _____

'The amount of blood pumped by the heart
is equivalent to three times the weight of
a whole person.'

e. David Attenborough talking about global warming: _____

'Dealing with global warming doesn't mean we have
all got to suddenly stop breathing. Dealing with global
warming means that we have to stop waste, and if you
travel for no reason whatsoever, that is a waste.'

Task 5 Indirect quotations or citations

Indirect quotations or citations report ideas or information from another source using your own words. Indirect quotations allow you to summarise important points from an acknowledged source.

A good indirect quotation attempts to extract the essence of the author's ideas and express them in the writer's own voice. A good note-taking technique is important. Using keywords, symbols, paraphrasing (*giving the meaning in another form*) and summarising (*expressing ideas in a concise form*) at the note-taking stage makes it less likely that you will copy by mistake.

Indirect quotations are used much more frequently than direct quotations in academic writing because they allow for greater flexibility and smoothness in our work.

> Example of an indirect quotation/citation
>
> *According to Attenborough (1984), we can tackle global warming by reducing waste, which includes unnecessary travel.*

5.1 **Has the writer paraphrased or summarised Attenborough's words? What is the difference?**

_____

_____

5.2 **Rewrite Attenborough's quotation using the following conventions.**

    a.   (Attenborough, 1984)

    _____

    _____

    b.   … argues that …

    _____

    _____

    c.   In a recent article, …

    _____

    _____

Task 6 Reporting verbs

In academic writing, we use reporting verbs such as *Szasz (1974)* **comments** *that ...*

There are many different reporting verbs, and each of them has a slightly different meaning, reflecting the author's stance.

6.1 **Match these reporting verbs (a–e) with the authors' stance (1–5).**

a.	suggests	1.	shows through evidence
b.	argues	2.	does not say directly
c.	demonstrates	3.	has a different opinion from someone else
d.	states	4.	does not have strong evidence
e.	implies	5.	says clearly and neutrally

promise decide remind offer promise threaten recommend agree accuse suggest deny admit insist warn advise blame explain refuse apologise decide insist invite encourage recommend congratulate

3

Task 7 Practice using indirect quotations

7.1 Discuss the quotation below and make sure you have understood what the author is saying. Then close your book and try to summarise the author's main point on conversation and silence using an appropriate reporting verb.

> According to Saville-Troike (1989):
>
> '… certain American Indian groups are accustomed to waiting several minutes in silence before responding to a question or taking a turn in a conversation. The native English speakers they may be talking to will have very short time frames (as little as four seconds) for responses or conversational turn-taking, finding silences embarrassing. The possibility for misunderstanding here is immense (p. 108).'

7.2 Compare your indirect quotation with other people in the class and decide who has best expressed Saville-Troike's ideas in their own words.

Reflect

Find an article from an academic journal which is of interest to you and count the number of direct and indirect quotations which the author uses.

Look at how the quotations are included in the text. What reporting verbs are used and why?

4   Reading and note-taking

At the end of this unit, you will be able to:

- take effective notes to avoid plagiarism
- paraphrase and summarise naturally

Research involves, among other things, reading books and articles which may be in journals or available on the internet. It is always helpful if you begin reading by knowing what it is you hope to find out.

Start with some questions. This will mean that, as you are reading, you will only note down information which is relevant to your questions. This method will reduce the temptation to copy down large sections of what you are reading in a relatively random fashion.

Task 1 Reading and note-taking

A student has been assigned an essay with the title:

'English has become a global language because it is easy to learn.' Discuss.

She makes a list of the questions before starting her research. They are:

- Is English easy to learn?
- Which languages are easier/more difficult than English?
- Does it depend on your first language as to whether English is easy to learn?
- Does it depend on what kind of learner you are as to whether English is easy to learn?

She finds two articles, given in full here on pages 24 and 25.

1.1   **Read the articles on pages 24–25 and take notes in your own words of any information which would help answer the questions.**

    a.   Is English easy to learn?

    b.   Which languages are easier/more difficult than English?

    c.   Does it depend on your first language as to whether English is easy to learn?

    d.   Does it depend on what kind of learner you are as to whether English is easy to learn?

1.2   **Use your notes in Task 1.1 to write one of the paragraphs *a*, *b* or *c* for the essay. Make sure you include an indirect quote.**

    a.   A paragraph on learner motivation and ease of language learning.

    b.   A paragraph on similarities and differences between languages.

    c.   An introduction to the essay.

Reflect

Did the exercise above make a difference to the way you read the articles? Why/Why not? Discuss with a partner.

'Some languages are harder than others'

Many people speak of languages as 'easy' or 'difficult', meaning that it is easy or difficult to learn these languages. People do not usually talk about their mother tongues as being easy or difficult for them as native speakers to use. Swedish schoolchildren may say that English is much easier than German 'because English does not have as much grammar'. Immigrants can be heard saying that English, Swedish, German or some other language is quite difficult. Linguists prefer not to comment on such matters globally. There is, they would say, no single scale from easy to difficult, and the degree of difficulty can be discussed on many levels.

The difficulty of learning a language as a foreign language refers to some kind of relative difficulty: how hard is it to get there from here?

The real question posed here, though, is whether some languages are simpler than others in some absolute sense, in terms of their own systems rather than in terms of some external perspective. It is quite obvious that it is easier for a Swede to learn Norwegian than Polish. For a Czech it is easier to learn Polish than Norwegian. Swedish and Norwegian are similar because they are closely related linguistically and also because they have existed in close cultural contact for several centuries. This means that if you have English as your mother tongue, it is easier to learn Germanic languages, like Dutch and German than it would be to learn Slavic languages, like Polish and Russian or Turkic languages, like Kazakh and Tatar. The major reason for this is that the vocabularies have so many similarities in both form and content in the related languages.

Let us look at the components of our linguistic knowledge, and let us assume that our knowledge of a language consists of the following three parts: grammar, vocabulary and rules of usage. This means that if you have English as your first language, you have an English grammar in your head. This grammar makes your pronunciation and your word order similar to that of other English speakers. You also have an English vocabulary at your disposal. You also have a number of rules of usage at your disposal. These rules tell you when to speak and when to keep quiet, how to address a person, how to ask questions and how to conduct a telephone conversation.

The difficult thing about learning a language is the vocabulary, whether learning one's native language or learning a foreign language. Each individual word is not difficult to learn, but when it is a matter of thousands of words, it does take a lot of time. We learn the grammar of our native language before we start school, but we work on our vocabulary as long as we live. Vocabulary is, then, the most difficult part and that which takes the longest time to learn.

For a language learner, the writing system and the orthography (rules for spelling) are major obstacles. Europeans have to spend a lot of time learning how to use the Arabic, Chinese or Japanese writing systems. Turkish, for example, was written in the Arabic script before 1928. Since then it has been written in the Latin alphabet. This, of course, makes it much easier for anyone accustomed to the Latin alphabet. As far as spelling is concerned, an orthography following the principle that there should be a one-to-one correspondence between sounds and letters is simpler than one not meeting this condition.

If we are looking for an absolute measure of linguistic simplicity, we should find it in the field of grammar. We can begin by considering the sound systems of languages. It must surely be the case that the fewer vowels, the fewer consonants and the simpler syllabic structure a language has, the simpler the sound system is. Hawaiian has 13 distinctive sounds ('phonemes' in linguistic terminology). According to a recently published description, a language spoken in southern Botswana has 156 phonemes, of which 78 are rather unusual sounds called 'clicks', 50 are ordinary consonants and 28 are vowels. Studies of other languages in the area have also arrived at phoneme counts of around 150. The sound systems of these languages are extremely complex. We can rest assured that the pronunciation of Hawaiian would be easier to learn than that of the Khoisan languages. We can also sum up by saying that it actually seems to make sense to place the languages of the world along a scale from simple sound systems to difficult. English takes a place near the middle of such a scale, where most of the languages of the world also crowd. Hence, most languages are equally difficult as far as the sound system is concerned, but there are some examples of considerably simpler and more difficult languages at this level.

There are a number of problems which are encountered when discussing the simplicity or difficulty of languages. This is because languages are not uniformly simple or difficult. Simplicity in one part of the language may be balanced by complexity in another part.

(Bauer and Trudgill, 1998, pp. 50–57)

'Learner differences'

The learner factors that can influence the course of development are potentially infinite and very difficult to classify in a reliable manner. Second language acquisition research has examined five general factors that contribute to individual learner differences in some depth. These are age, aptitude, cognitive style, motivation and personality.

A question that has aroused considerable interest is whether adults learn a L2 in the same way as children. A common-sense approach to this issue suggests that adult and child second language acquisition are not the same. First, it needs to be shown whether the learning route differs. Is there a 'natural' route for adults and a different one for children? Second, the rate at which adults and children learn needs to be investigated. The commonly held view that children are more successful learners than adults may not be substantiated by empirical research. It is possible, therefore, that differences exist with regard to both route and rate of learning.

Aptitude is to be contrasted with intelligence. The latter refers to the general ability that governs how well we master a whole range of skills, linguistic and non-linguistic. Aptitude refers to the special ability involved in language learning. The effects of aptitude have been measured in terms of proficiency scores achieved by classroom learners. A number of studies (e.g., Gardner, 1980) have reported that aptitude is a major factor in determining the level of success of classroom language learning.

Learner motivation and needs have always had a central place in theories of second language acquisition. Learners who are interested in the social and cultural customs of native speakers of the language they are learning are likely to be successful. Similarly, when learners have a strong instrumental need to learn a L2 (e.g., in order to study through the medium of the L2), they will probably prosper. Conversely, learners with little interest in the way of life of native speakers of the L2 or with low instrumental motivation can be expected to learn slowly and to stop learning some way short of native speaker competence. The role of motivation has been extensively examined in the work of Gardner and Lambert (1972) in the context of bilingual education in Canada and elsewhere.

Little is known about how personality and cognitive style influence second language acquisition although there is a general conviction that both are potentially extremely important. What kind of personality is most successful in learning a L2? Are extroverts more successful than introverts because they are prepared to take more risks and try to get more exposure to the L2? What role does inhibition play in second language acquisition? There are few clear answers. Similarly, research has not been able to show that cognitive style ('the way we learn things in general and the particular attack we make on a problem' Brown, 1980a, p. 89) affects learning in any definite way. One of the major problems of investigating both personality and cognitive style is the lack of testing instruments that can reliably measure different types.

(Ellis, 1985, pp. 210–211)

At the end of this unit, you will be able to:

- put into practice what you have learned

Task 1 Acceptable uses of external sources of information (books, journals, internet sites)

1.1 Out of the five approaches to using external sources in your academic work outlined below, only two are appropriate. Circle these two.

a. Putting quotation marks round a section taken from a website, indenting and single-spacing it if it is longer than a few lines (block style) and citing the source in text and in the reference list/bibliography.

b. Copying a section from a book word for word (verbatim), but not acknowledging the source either in text or in the reference list or bibliography.

c. Changing a few words for synonyms in a section taken from a journal and acknowledging the source in the reference list/bibliography, but not as an in-text reference.

d. Copying a section from a book word for word (verbatim) without quotation marks and putting a reference to the author at the end of the paragraph where you have included the words.

e. Expressing the ideas found in a journal article in your own voice and acknowledging the source of the ideas both in-text and in the reference list/bibliography.

Task 2 Who has got it right?

2.1 Three students want to use the following ideas found in a book in their respective essays on 'British culture'. Which student has incorporated the ideas correctly?

> 'In the UK, Christmas is traditionally seen as a time for "going home", a time for family and hearth. A modern trend is to go abroad, but usually to a more extreme winter climate in search of snow. Summer holidays are for "going away", abroad, if possible, to a more extreme summer climate where everything around us signifies heat. To stay at home during this period can only be justified on grounds of extreme poverty.' (Barley, 1989, p. 119)

a. **Student One:**

> Holidays appear to be very important to the British who seem to divide holidays into those that involve staying at home and those that require going away, summer being the time that most English people leave their homes unless they are very poor.

b. **Student Two:**

> In the cycle of life for the British person, holidays play an important role. Summer is a time for going away. To stay at home during this period can only be justified on grounds of extreme poverty. (Barley, 1989: 119)

c. **Student Three:**

> Holidays do not signify something in every culture, but for the British they are seen as extremely important events in the year, especially the summer holiday. According to Barley (1989), 'to stay at home during this period can only be justified on grounds of extreme poverty' (p. 119)

Reflect

Write a letter to a friend in your country who is coming to the UK to study, explaining what you have learned about referencing and plagiarism and how this might differ from practices in your country.

Web work

Website 1

Citing and referencing in the APA style

http://www.apastyle.org

Review

A valuable resource for information about correct formatting in the APA style of reference lists, bibliographies and citations.

Task

Watch slides 13 to 26 of 'The Basics of APA Style tutorial' and make notes on the format that you think you may need to use in writing your own reference lists.

Choose a source type in the 'Quick Answers' – References section and learn how to reference this type of source in the APA style.

Website 2

In-text citations: Author/Authors

https://owl.english.purdue.edu/owl/resource/560/03/

Review

A valuable resource for all things to do with academic writing.

Task

Make up a ten-question quiz based on the information presented on this webpage and try it out on your classmates.

Extension activities

Activity 1

List ten facts that are common knowledge that would not need to be referenced.

Activity 2

Prepare a poster warning students against plagiarism along the lines of an anti-smoking poster.

G

Glossary

access (a site) (v) To go to a website.

APA system (n) APA stands for the American Psychology Association which produces a citation style called the APA system. This is one of a number of citation styles which sets out how to reference sources in a bibliography or in the body of the text.

author (n) The person who writes a book, article or other printed text, electronic article or system, such as a website.

bibliography (n) A list of references to sources used by the author in a piece of academic writing or a book. A bibliography should consist of an alphabetical list of books, papers, journal articles and websites, and is usually found at the end of the work. It may also include texts suggested by the author for further reading. It differs from a reference list in that sources that are not cited in the body of the work, but were nevertheless used are also included.

cite (v) To acknowledge sources of ideas in your work. This may consist of an in-text reference to an author, a reference in a bibliography or footnote or a verbal reference in a talk or lecture.

conventions (n) Widely used and accepted practices that are agreed upon. Academic conventions for research include: dividing essays and reports into sections, referencing all sources and writing a bibliography according to certain styles, such as the APA System.

corporate author (adj) A term used to describe authorship of a text that does not have a named author (or authors), such as a report or article produced by a government department or other organisation.

digital object identifier (DOI) (n) A unique set of letters and numbers assigned to a particular article that enables quick access to the article online.

edition (n) All the copies of a version of a published text produced at one time are known as an edition. Later editions of a text may include changes, corrections and additions so, if known, it is necessary to state the edition of a text that you cite in a bibliography.

electronic source (n) Any text that has been accessed on the internet or from a CD or video, rather than from a printed source.

evaluate (v) To assess information in terms of quality, relevance, objectivity and accuracy.

format (n) The particular set of guidelines or rules which are to be used in presenting or organising certain information.

in-text reference (n) A reference that is in the body of the text. It is normally put in brackets and is shorter than the reference in the bibliography. It should include the author's name and the year of publication as a minimum.

journal (n) A publication that is issued at regular and stated intervals, such as every month or quarter, which contains articles and essays by different authors. Journals include magazines and newspapers as well as academic periodicals that contain more scholarly articles on specialised topics.

paraphrase (v) To alter a piece of text so that you restate it (concisely) in different words without changing its meaning. It is useful to paraphrase when writing a summary of someone's ideas; if the source is acknowledged, it is not plagiarism. It is also possible to paraphrase your own ideas in an essay or presentation; that is, to state them again, often in a clearer, expanded way.

plagiarism (n) The act of presenting someone else's work, i.e., written text, data, images, recording, as your own. This includes:

- copying or paraphrasing material from any source without an acknowledgement;
- presenting other people's ideas without acknowledging them;
- working with others and then presenting the work as if it was completed independently.

Plagiarism is not always deliberate, and it is important to adopt the academic conventions of always indicating ideas and work that are not your own, and referencing all your sources correctly.

publication (n) A body of written work, which is available for others to read and can be used as a source of information. For example, books, journals, newspapers and magazines. These may be in printed form or electronic form, for example, where they are available online.

quotation (n) A part of a text written or spoken by one author and reproduced in a text, piece of academic writing or talk by another author. When you quote someone's words or ideas, you do not change the wording at all and should put it in inverted commas ("~") to signal that it is a quotation.

reference (n) (v) 1 (n) Acknowledgement of the sources of ideas and information that you use in written work and oral presentations. 2 (v) To acknowledge or mention the sources of information.

reference list (n) An alphabetical list of sources used and cited in text by an author. The reference list usually appears at the end of the piece of work.

research (n) (v) 1 (n) Information collected from a variety of sources about a specific topic. 2 (v) To gather information from a variety of sources and analyse and compare it.

source (n) Something (usually a book, article or other text) that supplies you with information. In an academic context, sources used in essays and reports must be acknowledged.

unique resource locator (URL) (n) The address of a webpage that appears in the browser.

Published by
Garnet Publishing Ltd
8 Southern Court
South Street
Reading RG1 4QS, UK

Copyright © Garnet Publishing Ltd 2015

This book is based on an original concept devised by Dr Anthony Manning and Mrs Frances Russell.

ISBN 978 1 78260 182 1

British Library Cataloguing-in-Publication Data
A catalogue record for this book is available from the British Library.

Production

Project Manager:	Clare Chandler
Editorial team:	Clare Chandler, Kate Kemp
Design & Layout:	Madeleine Maddock
Photography:	Alamy, iStockphoto

Garnet Publishing and the authors of TASK would like to thank the staff and students of the International Foundation Programme at the University of Reading for their respective roles in the development of these teaching materials.

All website URLs provided in this publication were correct at the time of printing. If any URL does not work, please contact your tutor, who will help you find similar resources.

Printed and bound in Lebanon by International Press: interpress@int-press.com

Acknowledgements

Page 2: *A Handbook for Deterring Plagiarism in Higher Education* by Jude Carroll, reproduced with kind permission of Oxford Centre for Staff and Learning Development (OCSLD)

Page 4: By permission. From Merriam-Webster's Dictionary of Law ©2011 by Merriam-Webster, Inc. (www.Merriam-Webster.com).

Page 10: *NGOs, States, and Donors Revisited: Still Too Close for Comfort?* in World Development, Volume 66. Used under the CC-BA-SA 3.0 license, http://creativecommons.org/licenses/by-sa/3.0/legalcode.

Page 11: *Fisheries in transition: Food and nutrition security implications for the global South in Global Food Security*, Volume 3. Used under the CC-BA-SA 3.0 license, http://creativecommons.org/licenses/by-sa/3.0/legalcode.

Page 16: *The Second Sin* by Thomas Szasz (copyright © Thomas Szasz, 1973), reprinted by permission of A.M. Heath & Co Ltd.

Page 19: Quote from David Attenborough, reproduced with kind permission of *The Guardian*.

Page 22: *The ethnography of communication* by Muriel Saville-Troike, reproduced with kind permission of Blackwell Publishing.

Page 24: *Language Myths* by Laurie Bauer and Peter Trudgill, reproduced with kind permission of Penguin.

Page 25: *Understanding Second Language Acquisition* by Rod Ellis, reproduced with kind permission of Oxford University Press.

Page 27: *Native Land* by Nigel Barley, reproduced with kind permission of David Higham Associates.